THE DEER FAMILY

Published by Creative Education, 123 South Broad Street, Mankato, Minnesota 56001

Copyright © 1996 by Wildlife Education, Ltd. Copyright 1996 hardbound edition by Creative Education. All rights reserved. No part of this book may be reproduced in any form without written permission from the publisher. Printed in the United States.

Printed by permission of Wildlife Education, Ltd.

Library of Congress Cataloging-in-Publication Data

Biel, Timothy L.
The deer family / series created by John Bonnett Wexo: written by Timothy Levi Biel: zoological consultant, Charles R. Schroeder: scientific consultants, Leonard Lee Rue II, John E. Tanck.
    p.   cm. — (Zoobooks)
Includes index.
Summary: Examines the physical characteristics, habits, and natural environment of various species of deer, few of which live to be five years old.
ISBN 0-88682-775-2
1. Cervidae—Juvenile literature. [1. Cervidae. 2. Deer.] I. Title. II. Series: Zoo books (Mankato, Minn.)
QL737.U55B54   1996
599.73'57-dc20   95-45316   CIP AC

THE DEER FAMILY

Creative Education

Art Credits

Pages Eight and Nine: John Francis

Pages Ten and Eleven: John Francis

Page Eleven: Top, Lew Sadler; **Bottom,** Ed Zilberts

Pages Twelve and Thirteen: John Francis

Page Thirteen: Top, Carolyn Jagodits; **Middle,** Lois Sloan

Pages Sixteen and Seventeen: John Francis

Page Seventeen: Top, Graham Allen; **Middle,** Raul Espinoza; **Bottom,** Walter Stuart

Pages Eighteen and Nineteen: John Francis

Page Nineteen: Top, Rebecca Bliss; **Bottom,** Walter Stuart

Pages Twenty and Twenty-One: John Francis

Page Twenty-One: Bottom, Lois Sloan

Photographic Credits

Front Cover: Erwin and Peggy Bauer (*Bruce Coleman, Inc.*)

Pages Six and Seven: Tom and Pat Leeson (*Photo Researchers*)

Page Eight: Top, K.W. Fink (*Ardea London*); **Middle Left,** Wardene Weisser (*Bruce Coleman, Inc.*); **Bottom,** Jane Burton (*Bruce Coleman, Ltd.*)

Page Nine: Top Left, Stephen Krasemann (*Peter Arnold, Inc.*); **Middle,** G.C. Kelley; **Bottom,** Michael Leach (*Natural History Photos*)

Page Twelve: Middle Left, Michael Ederegger (*DRK Photo*); **Middle,** Grant Heilman; **Middle Right,** David C. Fritts; **Bottom,** Tom and Pat Leeson

Page Thirteen: Top, Bruce Curtis (*Peter Arnold, Inc.*); **Middle Left,** Richard Mackson (*Alpha/FPG*); **Middle Right,** Richard Leonhardt; **Bottom,** Kenneth Fink (*Ardea London*)

Pages Fourteen and Fifteen: Kennan Ward (*Bruce Coleman, Inc.*)

Page Sixteen: Top Right, David C. Fritts; **Bottom,** James R. Fisher (*Photo Researchers*)

Page Eighteen: George W. Calef (*Photo Researchers*)

Page Nineteen: Top Left, Leonard Lee Rue; **Middle,** Tom and Pat Leeson

Page Twenty-One: Left, Leonard Lee Rue (*Shostal Associates*); **Middle,** Shostal Associates; **Right,** Lynn Rogers

Pages Twenty-Two and Twenty-Three: Steven Fuller (*Animals Animals*)

Our Thanks To:
Deanna Leonhardt; Bernard Thornton (*Linden Arts Ltd.*); Andy Lucas; Pam Stuart; Karen Morris (*Maine's Inland Fisheries and Wildlife Department*); Dr. Dickson J. Phiri (*Mesa College*); Larry Killmar (*San Diego Wild Animal Park*); Michaele Robinson; Anga Biel

Cover Photo: Mule deer

Contents

The deer family is one of the most successful families of large mammals in the world. At one time, deer only lived in Asia. And there are still more different kinds of deer in Asia than on any other continent.

But deer have spread throughout the world. Europe has its roe deer, red deer, and fallow deer. North America has the whitetail, blacktail and mule deer. In western North America, you will find gigantic moose and elk. Farther north, huge herds of *caribou* (CARE-UH-BOO) trek across the frozen tundra. And in the south, many smaller deer, some barely a foot tall (30 centimeters), live in the jungles of Central and South America.

Despite this variety, all members of the deer family have many things in common. They are strictly plant eaters. They have hooves on their feet. They have slender bodies and long thin legs. Their hair is brown. And most male deer have *antlers* on their heads. These bony "branches" are a unique characteristic of deer. No other animal in the world grows antlers.

Most male deer are called *bucks*, and females are called *does*. Baby deer are usually known as *fawns*. However, we do not use these names when talking about moose, elk, or caribou. We talk about these large deer as if they were cattle! We call the males *bulls*, the females *cows*, and the young *calves*.

One reason for the success of deer is that they are great "athletes." They are strong, fast, and graceful. One second a deer can be standing still, and the next second it will be running *45 miles per hour* (72 kilometers per hour). It can even dodge boulders and trees without slowing down. It can leap across streams 30 feet (9 meters) wide and jump over fences 10 feet (3 meters) high. And a deer makes all these things look easy!

But life in the wild is not easy. Wolves, coyotes, tigers, cougars, and many other animals hunt deer. In the winter, deer have a hard time finding food. Few live to be five years old. But a whitetail doe in New Jersey once lived more than 20 years. And somewhere in the world, there is probably a wise buck that has been outsmarting its enemies even longer.

Although moose live for 20 to 25 years, by the age of 8, a male moose has his best antlers. This bull moose was photographed in Alaska, where the moose grow especially large.

7

Different kinds of deer live in forests and meadows throughout the world. There are about 40 species of deer, and in some ways, they all look alike. They have long necks, slender bodies, and long, thin legs. They have big eyes and ears, and hooves on their feet. Most male deer have antlers.

But every species is different. There are deer with big antlers, deer with small antlers, and deer with no antlers at all. Some deer have spots, and some do not. There is also a wide range of sizes. As you will see, all these differences help deer to live in different places around the world.

RED BROCKET DEER *Mazama americana*

MUNTJAC OR BARKING DEER *Muntiacus muntjak*

This little deer has very small antlers. But then, large antlers would just be a nuisance in the dense forests of southeast Asia, where the muntjacs live. These unusual deer have a strange way of protecting themselves. When they see a predator, they make a deep noise that sounds like a dog barking. And they may keep "barking" for an hour or more!

Large deer usually live where the weather gets cold, because their bodies can hold heat for a long time. The biggest deer in the world is the North American moose (right). It may stand more than eight feet (2.4 meters) tall at the shoulders and weigh nearly a ton (900 kilograms). It lives in the mountains of western Canada and the northwestern United States.

MOOSE
Alces alces

CHINESE WATER DEER *Hydropotes inermis*

Millions of years ago, the earliest members of the deer family lived in Asia. They did not have antlers, but the males had small, sharp tusks, which they used for weapons. Today, there are deer that live along river beds in the jungles and grassy plains of China that still resemble their ancient ancestors. They have no antlers, but the males grow tusks, which they use for fighting.

The smallest deer in the world is the South American pudu (left). It is about one foot tall (.3 meters) and weighs less than 20 pounds (9 kilograms). It lives in the lower regions of the Andes Mountains. Like most little deer, it does not live where the weather gets too cold.

PUDU
Pudu pudu

8

Some species of deer, like the red brocket at left, live in the tropical jungles of Central and South America. Their small size helps them run through thick brush. Their beautiful dark hair helps them hide in the shady jungle.

BARREN-GROUND CARIBOU *Rangifer tarandus*

Caribou, or *reindeer*, are built to travel. Because they live so far north, they have to migrate south in the winter to find food. But they have strong, sturdy bodies so they can walk a long way, even on cold, snowy days. (Incidentally, reindeer *do* live near the North Pole, and they *are* used by some people for pulling sleighs!)

ROCKY MOUNTAIN ELK *Cervus elaphus*

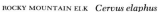

Elk once roamed over most of North America. From season to season, these huge deer wandered in great herds looking for food. The large herds of elk needed plenty of food and lots of wide open space. Today, the only places where elk can find enough food and space are in the rugged mountain areas of western Canada and the northwestern United States.

FALLOW DEER *Cervus dama*

Most deer only have spots when they are young. But some species, like the fallow deer at right, keep their spots for life. Their white spots make them hard to see in the tall grass where they usually hide.

9

The strong, graceful body of a deer is built for living in a dangerous world. On its long, thin legs, a deer can outrun wolves and mountain lions. It can turn and jump at top speed, even in a dense forest.

If it has to, the deer can defend itself, too. Its hard, pointed hooves can deliver a painful kick. And if nothing else works, a male deer may use its antlers to fight off an attacker.

But speed is still its best defense, and a deer will always run from danger if it gets the chance. That is why deer have excellent senses—to warn them when danger is near.

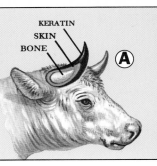

Antlers are different from *horns* Ⓐ. A horn is built to stay on forever. There is a bone inside the horn, which is permanently attached to the skull. This bone is covered by a thin layer of skin. Over the skin is a tough, outer layer of *keratin*, the substance in your fingernails.

KERATIN
SKIN
BONE
Ⓐ

With such skinny legs, you wonder how a deer can even stand up. But these legs are packed with long muscles that are perfect for running. They help the deer take long, graceful strides. And that's why it can run so fast.

A deer's foot has four toes. Can you find them? The two small, outside toes are called *dewclaws*. And the two middle toes form the *hoof*. The hoof is covered by an extra tough, thick toenail. This allows the deer to run its fastest, because it is running on its tiptoes.

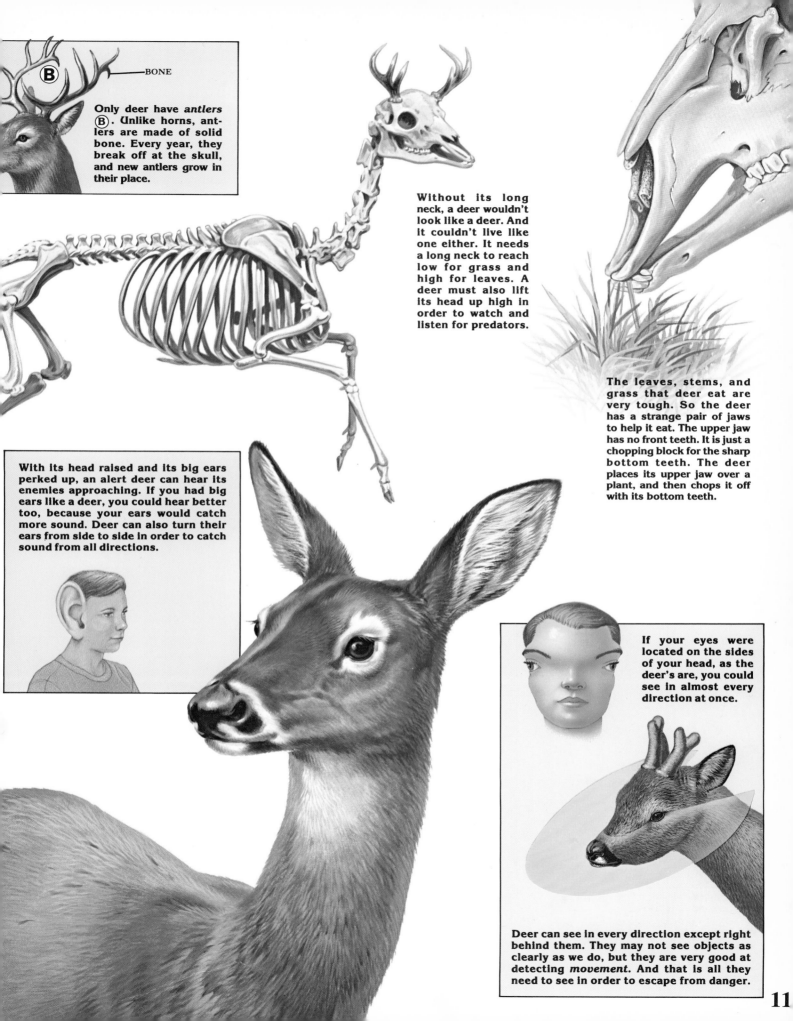

Only deer have *antlers* Ⓑ. Unlike horns, antlers are made of solid bone. Every year, they break off at the skull, and new antlers grow in their place.

—BONE

Without its long neck, a deer wouldn't look like a deer. And it couldn't live like one either. It needs a long neck to reach low for grass and high for leaves. A deer must also lift its head up high in order to watch and listen for predators.

The leaves, stems, and grass that deer eat are very tough. So the deer has a strange pair of jaws to help it eat. The upper jaw has no front teeth. It is just a chopping block for the sharp bottom teeth. The deer places its upper jaw over a plant, and then chops it off with its bottom teeth.

With its head raised and its big ears perked up, an alert deer can hear its enemies approaching. If you had big ears like a deer, you could hear better too, because your ears would catch more sound. Deer can also turn their ears from side to side in order to catch sound from all directions.

If your eyes were located on the sides of your head, as the deer's are, you could see in almost every direction at once.

Deer can see in every direction except right behind them. They may not see objects as clearly as we do, but they are very good at detecting *movement*. And that is all they need to see in order to escape from danger.

11

Antlers are one of nature's strangest creations. It takes a male deer four or five months to grow a pair of antlers. During this time, he must eat plenty of the right foods just to make them grow. And then, after he carries them around for six or seven months, they fall off! Yet every year without fail, the deer grows a new pair.

Antlers aren't easy to carry around, either. Can you imagine carrying an *80-pound* (36-kilogram) *weight* on top of your head wherever you go? That's how much a bull moose's antlers may weigh. And they may stretch *seven feet* (2.1 meters) from tip to tip!

You may wonder why a deer goes to all this trouble. But as you will see, the advantages of a good-looking pair of antlers outweigh the trouble it takes to grow them. And among most deer, the way antlers *look* is more important than the way they are used.

TRUE OR FALSE? **You can tell how old a male deer is by counting the number of points on his antlers.**

ANSWER: False. You can get *some idea* whether he is young or old, but the growth of a deer's antlers depends on many things. It depends, for example, on how healthy the deer is and how well it has been eating.

The male blacktail deer above Ⓐ is an unhealthy, poorly fed buck. That is why it has spindly little antlers. The buck at right Ⓑ is only a year old, but its sturdy antlers show that it is healthy. The large antlers with several points on the deer below Ⓒ, are a sign that this is a healthy, mature buck.

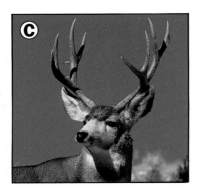

Every spring, a male deer begins to grow a new pair of antlers. The antlers start from two permanent stumps of bone on the deer's head ①. While they are growing, the antlers are soft and tender. They are covered with a thin skin called *velvet* ②. The velvet contains thousands of blood vessels, which carry calcium and other minerals for building strong bones.

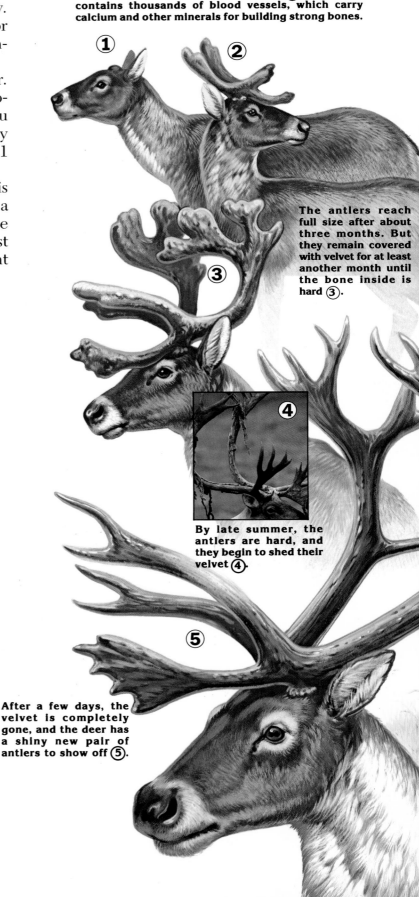

The antlers reach full size after about three months. But they remain covered with velvet for at least another month until the bone inside is hard ③.

By late summer, the antlers are hard, and they begin to shed their velvet ④.

After a few days, the velvet is completely gone, and the deer has a shiny new pair of antlers to show off ⑤.

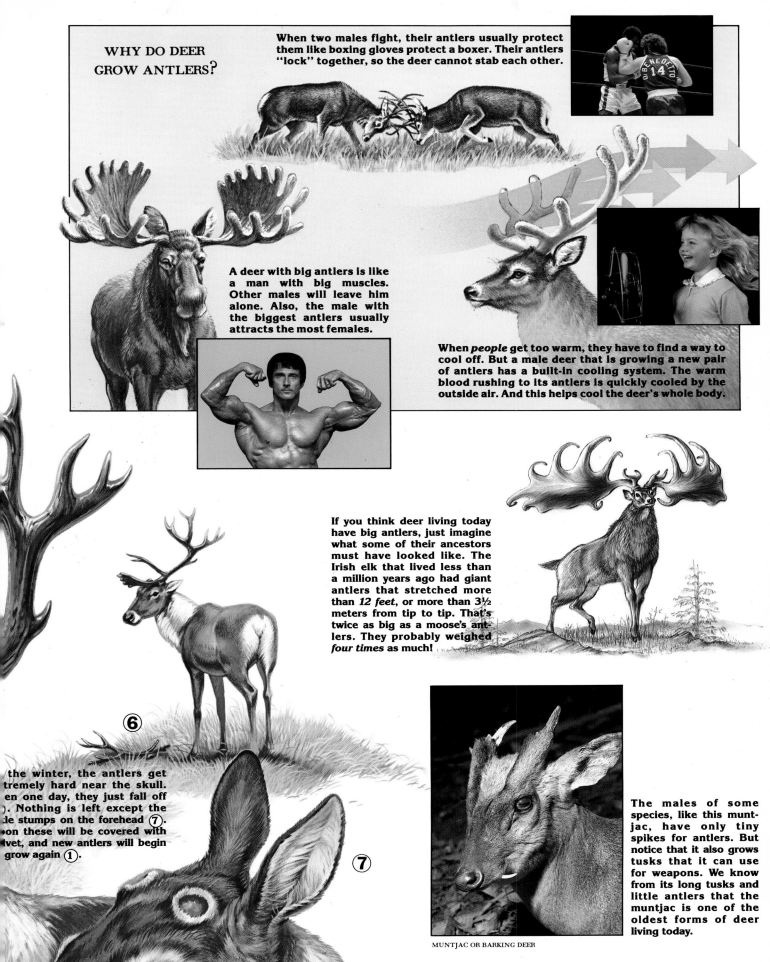

WHY DO DEER GROW ANTLERS?

When two males fight, their antlers usually protect them like boxing gloves protect a boxer. Their antlers "lock" together, so the deer cannot stab each other.

A deer with big antlers is like a man with big muscles. Other males will leave him alone. Also, the male with the biggest antlers usually attracts the most females.

When *people* get too warm, they have to find a way to cool off. But a male deer that is growing a new pair of antlers has a built-in cooling system. The warm blood rushing to its antlers is quickly cooled by the outside air. And this helps cool the deer's whole body.

If you think deer living today have big antlers, just imagine what some of their ancestors must have looked like. The Irish elk that lived less than a million years ago had giant antlers that stretched more than *12 feet*, or more than 3½ meters from tip to tip. That's twice as big as a moose's antlers. They probably weighed *four times* as much!

⑥

the winter, the antlers get tremely hard near the skull. en one day, they just fall off). Nothing is left except the le stumps on the forehead ⑦. on these will be covered with lvet, and new antlers will begin grow again ①.

⑦

The males of some species, like this muntjac, have only tiny spikes for antlers. But notice that it also grows tusks that it can use for weapons. We know from its long tusks and little antlers that the muntjac is one of the oldest forms of deer living today.

MUNTJAC OR BARKING DEER

13

Moose spend much of their time browsing, or selecting leaves and small plants for food. A moose might eat as many as 20,000 leaves a day.

14

Deer eat only plants. But they eat many different kinds of plants, depending on where they live and what season of the year it is. For example, moose live near water, and in the spring and summer, most of their food grows *underwater*. The female moose at right is using a rather unusual method to reach some weeds at the bottom of a pond.

No matter where a deer finds food, most of the plants it eats are hard to digest, because they are made of tough fibers. In order to eat them, the deer needs a very special stomach and an unusual digestive system.

WHITETAIL DEER

Long ago, deer could find all the food they needed in the forests and meadows where they lived. But today, that is not always true.

WHITETAIL DEER

Today, people have taken over much of the land that once belonged to deer and other wild animals. To keep from starving, many deer have to eat from farmers' fields. This whitetail deer has found a scrumptious meal in someone's corn fields.

In the summer, a moose can usually reach all the plants it wants simply by putting its head underwater. Sometimes, however, it will dive completely underwater just to get some food that looks especially good.

16

Different kinds of plants grow at different times of the year, so deer have to eat what is available. Follow this blacktail deer through all four seasons, and you will see some of the different foods it eats in a year.

In the spring, the deer finds plenty of juicy green leaves to eat Ⓐ.

Ⓐ

Ⓑ

In the summer, food is even more plentiful. In addition to leaves, the deer enjoys a banquet of herbs and mushrooms Ⓑ.

By autumn, most of the leaves and mushrooms have stopped growing. But the deer doesn't stop eating. It fattens up for the winter by munching on fallen acorns Ⓒ.

Ⓒ

Winter is the hardest time for deer. The ground is often covered with snow, so they must go to great lengths just to find a few leaves. Many of them do not survive, because there just isn't enough food to eat Ⓓ.

Ⓓ

Deer need *four stomachs* to digest the tough leaves and grasses that they eat! Actually, they have one big stomach divided into four sections called *chambers*. Before a deer's food can be completely digested, it has to go through all four chambers, as you see at right.

Feeding time is the most dangerous time for a deer. While it is looking for food, it is an easy target for predators. But its special stomach helps the deer to eat fast and escape. The first chamber of the stomach is like a big storage tank. The deer "fills its tank" quickly by gulping down as much food as this chamber will hold ①.

Then the deer can run and hide somewhere safe from predators ②.

When the deer is safe, it returns the food to its mouth in small bits called cud. The deer chews its cud slowly and then swallows it again. This time, the ground-up food goes to the second chamber, where it is digested even further ③.

After an hour or two in the second chamber, the food moves into the third and fourth chambers. There, over the next 20 hours, the food is completely digested and converted into fuel for the deer's body to use ④.

Herds of deer gather throughout the year for many different reasons. Some deer gather by the thousands so that they can migrate together. And smaller groups of deer gather to mate, care for their young, and stay safe from predators.

Just like groups of people, these deer need rules to keep peace and order in the herd. One rule is that the male deer with the biggest antlers is boss. Some deer, like the elk shown at right and below, even have rules for challenging the boss. These rules help prevent fights. And when fights do occur, they usually end before anyone gets hurt.

Elk usually live in herds. But males (*bulls*) and females (*cows*) stay in separate herds until the fall mating season. Then every bull tries to put together his own herd of cows. This herd is called a *harem*. A bull guards his harem carefully, so that other bulls do not steal his cows ①.

Sometimes one bull will challenge another bull and try to take over its harem. But as a rule, it will not challenge any bull with antlers larger than its own ②.

When a bull is challenged, it tries to scare the challenger away. It stretches out its neck and makes itself look fierce by shaking its antlers back and forth ③.

Finally, if neither one backs down, the bulls fight. First they circle each other like a pair of wrestlers. Then they bend their back legs, lower their heads, and charge! Sometimes they hit each other so hard that pieces of antlers go flying. They fight until one of them gives up and walks away. Then the winning bull claims the harem for himself ④.

BARREN-GROUND CARIBOU

Caribou form the world's largest herds of migrating deer. Twice a year, they gather by the thousands to make their seasonal journeys. In the winter, they head south to find food, sometimes traveling nearly 1,000 miles (1,600 kilometers). And in the spring, they return to their northern breeding grounds.

18

RED DEER

For elk and red deer, the mating season begins with a roar that can be heard for miles. This is the bull's way of announcing that he is "on the lookout" for females.

When migrating, caribou can be caught in terrible winter storms. But they know by instinct what to do. They nestle down in the soft snow. As cold as the snow is, it is warmer than the chilling wind. And it protects the caribou from the wind like an extra coat of fur. In their beds of snow, caribou wait out the storm.

Some deer do not live in herds. But they can still protect one another. For example, a whitetail doe will distract a predator that tries to attack her fawns. She runs back and forth in a crazy zigzag route to confuse the predator. And by taking long leaps, she leaves very little scent to follow.

WHITETAIL DEER

Not all male deer keep a harem of females. Many, like the bull moose below, follow behind a single cow. This gives the cow extra protection, because predators usually try to attack from behind.

④

A doe and her fawn are an adorable sight. A doe usually gives birth to one or two fawns in the spring. When they are born, most fawns, like the young roe deer below, are covered with white spots. This helps them hide in tall grass.

But when they are just a week or two old, the curious fawns begin following their mothers everywhere. As the fawns grow older, the mothers continue to protect them and help them find food, staying with them for at least a full year.

By then, the young deer are almost as tall as their mothers. Most of them have lost their spots, and young male deer are ready to grow their first antlers. When they are a year old, both males and females are ready to become independent adults.

A fawn spends its first week of life hidden in the grass. Its mother often feeds it and licks it clean, but then she leaves again. Because the fawn still has very little scent, it is safer without its mother nearby ①.

A mother must keep her newborn fawn safe from predators. She hides it in the grass and seems to lick it constantly. This keeps the fawn almost entirely free of scent.

①

Young deer, like young people, are very playful. And playing is important exercise. For deer, it helps them practice running fast to escape from their enemies. These young Chinese water deer are playing a game of chase.

Fawns do not remain helpless for long. They have to learn quickly how to walk and escape from predators. At the ripe old age of 20 minutes, this baby deer untangles its long legs and tries to stand up. After a few tries, it will succeed in taking its first wobbly steps (A).

B

By the time a fawn is two days old, it can stand up and walk without any trouble (B). At three weeks, it runs and jumps more gracefully than a ballet dancer (C).

C

A

WHITETAIL FAWN

QUESTION: Which of these two fawns is a male, and which is a female?

ANSWER: The fawn on the right is a male. You can tell because males have bony knobs on their foreheads. In another year, antlers will grow from these knobs.

After a week of hiding, the fawn is finally strong enough to accompany its mother. And for the next year, the two of them are always together (3).

The young fawn does not like to be left behind. When it is just a few days old, it tries to follow its mother wherever she goes. She may even have to force the fawn to lie down by pushing it gently with her foot (2).

Mothers and fawns stay together for at least a year. Then they go their separate ways (4). As long as it lives, a male fawn will probably not see its mother again. But young females often rejoin their mothers later. They even bring their own fawns with them and form small herds.

21

The future looks hopeful for many deer. In fact, the number of deer living in North America is on the rise. People have helped make this possible by working to preserve natural areas where deer can live. Unfortunately, this has not always been true. Before people learned the importance of protecting wildlife, they caused many species of deer to become extinct. And they seriously endangered many others.

The elk is a good example. Three hundred years ago, more than *10 million* elk roamed the plains of North America. But in just three centuries, people have destroyed much of the elk's natural habitat. They turned grazing lands into cities and farms. They built roads where elk once migrated. They chopped down forests where elk once hid. They also hunted and killed great numbers of elk.

Today, there are only a few thousand of these magnificent animals left. Several distinct types, or *races*, of elk have been lost forever. But people are trying to save those that are left. In some places they have established wilderness preserves. In others, logging and mining have been restricted so that the elk's natural habitat is not destroyed. As a result, the elk population has stopped its decline.

Some species of deer do not seem bothered by the changes humans have caused. Whitetail and blacktail deer have adapted so well that their numbers sometimes grow *too fast*. Then there isn't enough food to feed them all, and thousands of these deer starve to death.

People have made this problem worse by killing off most of the predators that hunt deer. Strange as it may seem, deer need predators to keep their population under control. But today, because there are so few natural predators left, humans have taken over that role. Through carefully controlled hunting, people can help to preserve a stable deer population.

Sadly, the future does not look so bright for the deer of Asia and South America, where people are chopping down trees and clearing away forests at an alarming rate. They sell the wood to build houses and use the cleared land for farms and villages. They are not leaving enough room for deer and other wild animals. Already, half the deer species on these continents are endangered. However, if people learn to manage their land and resources more carefully, most of these species of deer can be saved.

Most of the moose in North America live in remote areas. As a result, the species is safe from extinction for the time being.

Index